Beethoven Symphonies

Robert Simpson

ROBERT SIMPSON

BEETHOVEN
Symphonies

BBC MUSIC GUIDES

ARIEL MUSIC
BBC PUBLICATIONS

Published by BBC Publications
A division of BBC Enterprises Ltd
35 Marylebone High Street, London WIM 4AA

ISBN 0 563 20484 2

First published 1970
Reprinted 1973, 1975, 1976, 1978, 1979
First published in Ariel Music 1986

Typeset in 10/11 pt Garamond by Phoenix Photosetting, Chatham
Printed in England by Mackays of Chatham Ltd

Contents

Introduction

Some years ago Sir Malcolm Sargent set me thinking by casually remarking that if Beethoven's symphonies had been unnumbered and undated it might have been difficult to find out their correct order; the first two, he thought, would fall obviously into place and most people would guess that the Ninth was the last. The others, he said, might be in almost any order. I agreed with him, up to a point, when he confirmed that he really meant that with Beethoven what is usually called 'style' is not chronologically easily traceable by the usual methods, that it is in fact nothing but a function of his purpose, changing radically and rapidly as his purpose changes. In other words, the development of Beethoven's deeper purpose, artistic and human (the same thing with him), is itself organic throughout his life. Superficial talk about 'style' gets us nowhere. Beethoven's identity is shown by the supreme authority with which he directs and redirects his powers, rather than by personal fingerprints which, though they markedly exist, fade before the force of his humanity. In no other composer is this so strikingly evident. Most great composers, having once settled an individual way of expression, maintain it more materially than Beethoven, either within the scope of a definable period manner, like Bach, Handel, Haydn, or Mozart, or as a set of notably personal devices that remain fixed for life – Berlioz, Schumann, Chopin, Wagner, Liszt, Brahms, Bruckner, and many others. It is no doubt significant that Beethoven's historical position lies between these two opposite groups, but his achievement would not have been possible without unprecedented human power.

But we do know the proper order of the symphonies, and there is no reason why we should not take advantage of this knowledge for the sake of insight. If we do, we can come upon some rather startling surmises about Beethoven's development. Consider first the C minor and *Pastoral* symphonies; at their first performances (in the same concert) they were numbered respectively 6 and 5. These numbers are now reversed, and the C minor was in fact begun even before No. 4, which interrupted it in mid-course. Two reasons are usually suggested for this: (1) that the Fourth reflects the composer's happiness at his engagement to Therese von Brunswick (an event by no means attested), for the time being making it impossible for him to work at the stern C minor, and (2) that he may have felt it some sort of error of judgement to follow the gigantic *Eroica* directly with another epic. Both explanations seem dubious. Outward events, even of a personally affecting kind, had little immediate influence on Beethoven's music: we need think only of how, when he was depressed almost to the point of suicide, his musical faculty gave off the brilliant and confident Second Symphony. And we cannot assume that he felt it wrong to follow one heroic symphony with another, for he was not, after all, writing only symphonies. In 1805, when the C minor was begun, he was also composing the Fourth Piano Concerto, whose mysteriously serene first movement is based on much the same rhythm that opens the symphony so violently. Opposing aspects of the same thing, perhaps. But this piano concerto, together with the one for violin, he could have regarded even more aptly than the Fourth Symphony as a foil between the *Eroica* and C minor symphonies. It seems likely that a somewhat deeper consideration determined the order of Nos. 4, 5, and 6.

The first three symphonies show a continuous process of physical expansion that could go no further without threatening a looser kind of romantic exaggeration alien to Beethoven's nature. Having used the full power of his muscles in the *Eroica*, his instinct was to concentrate his new strength in denser discharges. The C minor symphony would be the obvious vehicle; he would demonstrate that he was now able not only to span vast territories but also to pack confined spaces with unheard-of concentration. By the end of 1805 the first two movements of the C minor (which was intended to be No. 4) were finished. Here he was faced with a problem; we know it was a troublesome matter because of his uncertainty concerning the repeat of scherzo and trio (discussed further on pp. 34–6). He knew that the work must have no ordinary scherzo, that this movement must be somehow magnetic and dramatic, and that the finale must be the most enormous blaze hitherto ignited in music. There matters halted. Meanwhile the idea for the B flat major symphony (the actual No. 4) came to him, and it seems to have been written fast – no extensive sketches are known. But the work is highly compact, as the C minor was going to be, yet lighter in character, as if Beethoven, unsure how to release the thing that roared in his head like a caged tiger, turned his attention to less obstreperous inhabitants of his extraordinary domain. If the *Eroica* is like a noble stallion, the C minor and B flat symphonies might be thought of as belonging to the cat family, the one fierce, the other lovable, but both sharing a compact suppleness of movement, a dangerous lithe economy that makes them akin and, together, different from their predecessor. The Fourth belongs to the Fifth – and never so much as in the Stygian darkness of its introduction, abruptly obliterated by vivid light.

About the same time, while the Fifth was laid by, Beethoven also composed the three Razumovsky quartets: the third of these begins, like the Fourth Symphony, with a strange hushed introduction that gives way to brilliant sunlight. By 1807 he felt he could resume work on the C minor. Even so, he seemed scarcely aware that the interruption was in the nature of a preparation, for the earliest version had the scherzo and finale separated, the former ending forte. Then it dawned on him; the final appearance of the scherzo was reduced in length and to pianissimo, creating space for a long, dark, breathless link to the finale. So did he pluck, dramatically, the fruit of the seed sown in the B flat symphony and the C major quartet. Clearly the idea did not occur to Beethoven without the intervening experience of the introductions to two quite different works.

There is a sequel to this particular story. These mysterious quiet slow introductions having engendered the link between scherzo and finale of the Fifth Symphony, Beethoven now sees another possibility, a further development and transformation of character hardly conceivable in any other composer. In the Sixth Symphony he takes advantage of the illustrative side of the work to devise a corresponding passage that blends surprisingly the functions of link, introduction, and a certain independence of form and character. The storm in the Pastoral Symphony is not only a link between scherzo and finale; it is a vast *allegro* introduction, both in its dramatic relationship to the finale and in its internal processes. Yet it stands as a separate (though not separable) part of the whole scheme, strongly contrasted in every possible way with the rest of the work, so that the listener tends to accept it as a distinct movement in its own right. One of Beethoven's most magnificent attainments is his creation of the phenomenon whose different aspects are almost exclusive of each other. If we consider the storm as a link, its function as an introduction virtually disappears, and vice versa; if we think of it as a separate movement, its other functions are apt to escape the ear. Such ambivalent phenomena can be found in many of Beethoven's later works and are always at once mysterious and clear; their discovery is always both baffling and revealing. We see what is done – but how could it have been done?

The storm has even another aspect: not only is it a separate movement, link, introduction – it is an interruption that is the entire reason for the relaxation of the finale. In the Fifth the link-passage, frozen into black immobility, explodes into a fiery finale; in the Sixth a furiously active link, introduction, interruption (what you will) is the cause of an essentially static relaxed rondo. The accomplishment in No. 6 would not have been possible without the experience of No. 5, in turn fathered by the introductions to No. 4 and the C major Razumovsky Quartet. Who would suppose such tempestuous music, still the greatest musical painting of its kind, would have arisen from such ancestry? But the whole process, when we look into it, is continuous, unpredictable, and inevitable.

In the light of all this there can be no doubt that the Sixth represents a slightly later stage than the Fifth. The Fourth, Fifth, and Sixth prove to be an interrelated group, and their chronological numbering is confirmed by internal evidence. Later (p. 51 ff.) we shall notice certain fascinating and basic similarities in the apparently disparate Seventh and Eighth symphonies, but at this point we must observe that there are (very roughly) three kinds of Beethoven symphony. The first two symphonies constitute one kind, springing directly from the eighteenth-century type that exists for its own and our musical delight, this its only continuing motivation, the character rooted in Beethoven's experience of other music but nevertheless unmistakably personal. In it we find a new scale of harmonic and tonal values dominating thematic individuality; the plainness of Beethoven's themes throws into relief the tonal architecture even more strikingly than in Mozart's most schematic works, where the harmonic horizons are narrower. In Beethoven's second type (if 'type' is a word we can ever use in connection with him) clearly describable extra-musical influences are at work; the Third, Fifth, Sixth, and Ninth obviously belong here, with the Fourth finely poised on a line between this and the first type and, as we have seen, performing with the Fifth a fascinating kind of symbiosis. The extra- (or perhaps supra-) musical elements in these works must not be overrated or misconstrued; Beethoven is still as concerned with perfection and depth of organisation as Bach — the fifty-odd chords of C major at the end of No. 5 are carried by a momentum so exquisitely controlled that anyone who does not feel their perfect punctuality has not yet understood the possibilities of classical music.

Only the Seventh and Eighth symphonies remain; they alone form a third category in which there is a curious self-sufficiency, a freedom from external connotations that might be thought to link them with the early type; yet their immense impact is itself as dramatic as any power of extra-musical suggestion. These two works share a certain leathery toughness of consistency; their rough-hewn severity, preoccupation with dynamic rhythmic development, and their often defiant humour could be blended only by one whose experience had taught him some harsh lessons. Theirs is an astringent maturity past its central phase of relaxed assurance; they have a weather-beaten look that could come only at a certain time of life. The iron authority behind such music could be attained only after the creation of many works of openly explicit emotional nature. The Ninth Symphony, though it must be placed with those works in which non-musical influences are explicit, would have been impossible without the Seventh and Eighth, both of which anticipate it in some profound ways. No matter how deeply we examine Beethoven's music we shall find that the growth of his art is uniquely consistent in its power of radical yet organic change. We cannot speak of the development of his 'style' – only of his growing control of power that can be directed with complete and unpredictable certainty.

The First Two Symphonies

Beethoven's harmonic scale is the main dimension distinguishing his early masterpieces from the mature ones of Haydn and Mozart. This does not mean, of course, that in all other respects he resembles them, any more than they resemble each other. Beethoven was aware of the new harmonic dimension, and also of his own marked individuality, that could show itself in themes and colouring with equal distinction. He often rejoiced in cladding the new structures with a wealth of individual invention, texture, and wit, in the quartets of Op. 18 and the early piano sonatas. With the symphony, however, architectural considerations came first; those of Beethoven's admirers who, delighted by the overt originality of the chamber music, expected a first symphony bristling with electrifying wizardry, must have been puzzled by its seeming plainness. But the symphony is cautious only in its subject-matter, which is designed to withstand big harmonic strains, and by its simplicity to draw attention from itself to the large lines. Beethoven suggests size from the outset in a new way, and this can be seen by comparing the opening of his first *allegro* with those of two more mature works by Mozart and Haydn. Mozart, in his last symphony (No. 41, in C major), proceeds at first, and characteristically, by exquisitely balanced phrase and counterphrase, conversational question and answer, observation and comment; the basis of C major is comfortably settled, and no expansion is even hinted:

Ex. 1

It is only later that we become aware that this music is assuming symphonic proportions. Like Mozart, Haydn in his Symphony No. 97, in the same key, concentrates on short figures which do not in themselves suggest expansiveness. Both composers, of course, show later that these figures have more of such power than one might at first have suspected, but even the aggressive irregularity of Haydn does not break away from the tightness with which the tonic grips it (Ex. 2 opposite).

Beethoven, by stepping up the harmony a tone in the seventh bar and by inserting two extra pairs of purely harmonic bars with glorious stretching effect, quietly makes one aware of a new scale of thought (Ex. 3).

Ex. 2

Once we are aware of this fundamental power of suggestion in Beethoven, we can no longer wish to question the use of thematic formulae. Beethoven's apparent caution is really boldness, though he is careful not to obscure its real origin by over-emphasising incidental strokes. Replace the introduction of the First Symphony with that of the *Prometheus* overture (both set out towards C from the dominant of F, but the latter much more theatrically) and the point becomes clear. We should never underestimate the first two symphonies. The remarkable harmonic shifts in the brilliant scherzo of No. 1 (still ironically called a minuet by the composer) are sometimes quoted as an isolated glimpse of the real Beethoven in a work otherwise conventional, but if we hear them aright their muscular contractions throw into relief the splendid and spacious relaxation of the rest. The use of open harmonic spaces in the trio, though less startling, is even more extraordinary in the context of its period, as also is the plain assertion of tonic formulae at the end of the first movement, where proportion is all. When Beethoven in the *andante* works with less exuberance a vein he had already discovered in

the corresponding movement of the C minor quartet, Op. 18 no. 4, he
is only being consistent in not wishing to distract the ear from the harmonic grandeur of the symphony, and at the same time achieving a far
higher degree of concentrated development. If he seems content with
plainness of material we may be sure that the harmonic and tonal proportions are meant to engage us before everything else; the supreme
example of this in the symphonies is perhaps the introduction to No. 7,
which we shall consider later (pp. 45–8).

No one has ever written more individual or beautiful themes than
Beethoven; where necessary he displays a power of self-denial that
should not mislead anyone, and Stravinsky's remark that he lacked the
gift of melody was surely a missile thrown from inside a glass house.
Economy is one of Beethoven's chief aims in No. 1, harmonic and
thematic; every movement has an unusual thematic density. I do not
subscribe very readily to the tendency to analyse over-ingeniously the
thematic content of classical works (a tendency created by serialism),
but would quarrel with no one who drew attention to the amount of
invention that seems, in the first movement, to grow from the little
downward gruppetto that introduces the main theme – at first:

Ex. 4

then broadening:

Ex. 5

and always broadening:

Ex 6

being combined with its own expansion:

Ex. 7

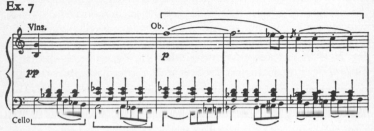

Now the climax of the exposition can employ freely descending phrases on a large scale without fear of *non sequitur*:

Ex. 8

And from this comes the cadential phrase, with its linking and equally apt slow woodwind descent (*b*):

Ex. 9

The crowning perceptiveness on Beethoven's part is that all this expansive descending would make the original gruppetto seem ludicrous if it were to bring about the repeat: so it is omitted, a tiny stroke of genius confirming a large one, and incidentally enabling Beethoven to strengthen the rhythm of the main theme itself as it returns. Each movement of this symphony will bear this kind of discussion (the use of scales in the insufficiently respected finale, for instance, is more subtle than appears at first sight), and intimacy with the work makes it more and more obvious that Beethoven was proving much to himself that untrammelled individuality of themes would have confused at this stage in his development. A similar situation arose later in his struggle with concerto form, won by the same means in the Triple Concerto.

Having realised that Beethoven's First Symphony is already a new type, we are in a position to grasp the greater dimensions of the Second. If we accept (as suggested on p. 10) that the first two symphonies belong to the eighteenth century in that their motivation is entirely musical, we must hear clearly that beneath the formal gestures and the fact that much of the material is from common stock a new kind of life is stirring; that it is, in fact, manifest. The thrilling *élan* of the Second Symphony is caused by the way Beethoven propels the thematic tags of his forefathers upon a tonal current of unprecedented breadth and force. A first movement of considerable power and size rises from the largest slow introduction yet composed by anyone; not even Mozart's Prague Symphony displays a prelude of such scope and variety, ranging from simple lyricism to an imposing D minor unison climax prophesying the Ninth Symphony. The massive and radiant culmination of the *allegro con brio* has, as Tovey says,[1] a choral quality that comes from 'The Heavens are telling' in Haydn's *Creation*, but it is only because Beethoven has given new emphasis and breadth to the harmonic and tonal aspects of the movement as a whole that he is able to create with the orchestra alone an effect hitherto obtainable only by means of choral resources. Such a climax grafted on to a Mozart or Haydn movement would be grossly disproportionate; here it is the only possible upshot. Later in life Beethoven is able to do more and more by power of suggestion, and there is a notable anticipation of this in the finale of this symphony; there the coda is neither so solid nor so weighty as in the first movement, yet the sense of climax is no less. This is due to the magical pianissimo interruptions on the edge of foreign keys which at once enlarge our conception of the world. Grove must have sensed this when he wrote, 'It is as if, after the chord of F sharp, we had passed through a door and were in a new, enchanted world' (see bar 336 *et seq.*).[2] This passage is often quoted as a mirage of Beethoven's so-called second period seen from his first; there is truth in that, but we should also note that the sudden enormous fortissimo at bar 372 is the point the music *would have reached much*

1 Sir Donald Tovey, *Essays in Musical Analysis*, Vol. 1 (OUP).
2 Sir George Grove, *Beethoven and his Nine Symphonies* (Novello and OUP).

later had it proceeded by the method of the coda of the first movement. Here power of suggestion is everything, and it is highly significant that it occurs in a movement where Beethoven allows himself complete freedom in the matter of individual themes. A formula such as this in the first movement

Ex. 10

demands accumulation of weight in its treatment, as well as broad (but subtle) rhythmic organisation in the movement as a whole. A totally different individual firework of a theme such as starts the finale

Ex. 11

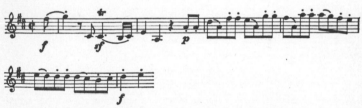

carries already within itself more than a suggestion of high contrast and makes possible the use of such contrasts, on a larger scale, as the means of screwing up tension and suggesting, rather than literally constructing, cumulative effects. This finale is full of inner and outer contrasts: there is violent humour, organ-like polyphony, and sheer orchestral brilliance, all in the first fifty bars; and what happens after that is anything but predictable, schematically as well as in detail. That it is all immensely coherent is due to Beethoven's power of suggestion at every minutest stage.

The scherzo anticipates this remarkable finale by employing fierce confrontations of dynamics and ideas; it is the first time Beethoven has used the title 'scherzo' in a symphony and, although the term has become generic, he uses it only when conscious of specific humorous or gay intention. He does not, for instance, employ it in the Fifth or Ninth symphonies, where there is no joke (the literal meaning of the word). Between the extremes of the formal magnificence of the first movement and the fierce wit of the last two lies the gloriously lazy expansiveness of the *larghetto*, a miracle of leisurely grace in extravagantly full sonata form. Yet there is no incongruity; Beethoven is already the greatest master of large-scale contrasts hitherto known. As this work unfolds itself we become increasingly aware of the internal use of Beethoven's power of suggestion; this is what confused its first hearers, and in referring to contemporary criticisms Grove amusingly remarks, 'the work is always spoken of more or less with hesitation, and as not so *safe* as No. 1'. But the composer is safely on the way to the *Eroica*.

Symphony No. 3, in E Flat Major (Eroica)

The process of expansion continues. I have already touched upon Beethoven's power of suggestion, and it is this that halts a tendency that might otherwise have interpreted expansion in purely physical terms. The fact that the *Eroica* is considerably longer than No. 2 is not the only sense in which it is larger. Tovey has demonstrated how Beethoven, by introducing a sudden series of remarkable modulations into a very solid fugue in the *Gloria* of the Mass in D, creates a sense of expansion that is in fact caused by a contraction, and we have noticed something of the kind in the finale of the Second Symphony. It is rather like the experience to be had in a small room when a window is suddenly opened to reveal a vast landscape. It is not necessary to explore the whole landscape to appreciate this particular effect on the imagination; a glimpse is better. Beethoven's mastery of the inspired glimpse and its perfect timing is absolute; if we could count the instances of it in the *Eroica* we should see how much larger is the work than its physical dimensions, huge though they are. This is one of the deeper meanings of expansion as Beethoven effects it. Referring to the *adagio* of the D minor Piano Sonata, Op. 31 no. 2, Tovey remarks that slowness means bigness.[1] This is true, but bigness does not necessarily mean slowness. The romantic period created in many minds the assumption that expansion inescapably entailed the slowing-down of music; with Beethoven expansion often means filling a larger time-scale with more, not less, activity.

The first movement of the *Eroica* is as ceaselessly mobile and concentrated a piece of high-pressure activity as has ever been generated; yet it is one of the longest first movements in existence. Vital energy could impel no greater athleticism than here, and the music never outruns its strength. This composition is 'slower' than its precursors only because its great moments of tension and relaxation are more widely spaced; in this sense its outlines are broader and it takes longer for the listener to absorb its processes. But the intervening stretches are packed with varied incident and action. The tempo is quick and must remain consistent so that we hear that it is Beethoven (and not the egotistical conductor) who is able to fluctuate the pace of his thought.

Confirmation that the composer requires a quick tempo for this first movement may be found in the fact that he was finally insistent on the repeat of its exposition, once taken out and then restored. (Evidence of

1 Sir Donald Tovey, *A Companion to Beethoven's Pianoforte Sonatas* (OUP).

this nature is more valid than the metronome marks, which are often too fast, as if Beethoven's machine were running slow.) He must have been afraid the movement would be too long, acutely aware that nothing of its size had been written before. But there are other more subtle reasons why this repeat is necessary; he did not explain them at the time. (Why should he? – he would have preferred, I am sure, to postpone rather than anticipate the present-day need of composers to provide elaborate explanations of their works.) Two at least of these reasons can be discovered by anyone who knows enough about Beethoven's methods. One is that he normally repeats his exposition when he intends to open his development with other than first-subject material, a point made during some brilliant broadcast talks by Peter Stadlen.[1] The *Eroica* is such a case, but the other reason is still more compelling – without the repeat, the fine rhythmic organisation of the whole movement is thrown slightly out of true. Consider the first two bars; these powerful detached chords must be introductory, since they cannot rhythmically be scanned with what immediately follows them. This is why some conductors have rather thoughtlessly avoided playing them in the main tempo. But though they stand apart at first, they nevertheless belong to the rhythmic whole – in a very long-term sense that can be satisfied only by playing the repeat. If we scan accurately the rhythmic periods of the music all the way to the double bar we find that at the repeat the two *forte* staccato E flat chords are replaced by two *pp* bars (the first two in the '1st time' bracket):

Ex. 12

These same two bars also herald the development (see the '2nd time' bracket). The beginning of the symphony and the beginning of the repeated exposition balance each other rhythmically; the one is answered by the other. At the start of the development we have another odd pair of bars, again introductory in function, now disturbing the equilibrium once more. We therefore expect them to be balanced or

1   BBC Third Programme, 13 and 20 July 1959.

answered in due course, perhaps at the recapitulation. But there Beethoven deliberately deceives us. True, the two bars before the recapitulation form a dynamic contrast like those at the start of the movement. But far from being rhythmically intrusive, these two bars are the last two in a straightforward four-bar phrase, thus:

Ex. 13

So we have not been given a proper answer to the two extra bars that introduce the development. For that we have to wait until the start of the coda. Look at bars 555–6: Beethoven cunningly extends a softly held E flat for two extra bars at the very point where the balance must be restored:

Ex. 14

To cut the repeat of the exposition therefore renders these two apparently innocent bars meaningless, and the facts show that for Beethoven the question of repeats was, like everything else, a consideration in depth. In all his masterpieces there is but one repeat of whose rightness I am not entirely convinced, and that can be rendered convincing if we return to the original form of the work, as I shall attempt to show in dealing with the Fifth Symphony (see pp. 34–6).

An essay of this kind cannot embark on extended analysis, but there is one more important point to be made about the first movement of the *Eroica* because, so far as I know, it has never been made anywhere else. All commentators note with enthusiasm the new theme Beethoven introduces in E minor into the development:

Ex. 15

Those who try to explain this usually resort to ingenious thematic contortions, unable to face the possibility that it might be new. Its origin is not in fact thematic or harmonic, but rhythmic; unobtrusively pervasive in the movement, until it gives rise to this fine theme, is the rhythmic figure ♪ ♩ ♩♩, and Beethoven confirms its intimate connection with Ex. 15 by using it as a regular punctuation in the bass. But the chief impact of this idea is its newness, which is why the composer is at pains to free it from melodic associations, and to make it a beautiful and unforgettable melody in its own right. Its newness is the most powerful thing everyone has noticed about it, and it is the factor upon which its function depends. It is no mere whim; it exists at an early stage in the sketching and, moreover, in E minor, a key vastly remote from the tonic E flat.

In order to find out Beethoven's purpose and the artistic realism of its execution, we must first go back to the start of the development. The exposition has been on a large scale; if the development is going to be even more expansive it will be faced with the structural problem of how convincingly to re-establish the tonic at the reprise, after such discursiveness as it must inevitably traverse. It may at first seem paradoxical that the new theme in the remote key of E minor has anything to do with this – but it has, and everything depends on it.

The first and last thing we remember about this theme is that it is new. So that its newness shall seem the more strange, Beethoven puts it into a remote key. But we must be made to feel that the key is remote, not merely another tonality in a haphazard tour of the harmonic universe. How is this done? Look at the music from bar 160 onwards. Beethoven here makes a decisive move from the B flat major of the end of the exposition. He goes to the dominant of C. From here on he passes through various regions. The C major turns momentarily to minor (bar 178), then by semitones through C sharp minor (182) to D minor (186). Here the music broadens; D minor holds, then swings to G minor at bar 198. The harmonic rhythm tightens again and Beethoven races to a climax on a chord of E flat at bar 220. So far the tonalities have been on the sharp side of E flat. The chord of E flat at 220 is not a tonic, but the dominant of A flat. Using it as a pivot the composer now swings round to the flat side of the tonic; he goes naturally into A flat major, which is the home subdominant, and from there into F minor, where black clouds loom. The tonalities have therefore been wheeling round the hub of the tonic, but without touching it. So E flat is still the centre, subtly consolidated. The storm breaks, and when Ex. 15 appears in E minor it sounds as remote as it should, though we may not realise why.

This is the first stage of a gigantic process. The E minor theme turns to the equally remote key of A minor (292). Abruptly Beethoven brings in the main theme, *forte*, in C major (300) and with giant strides reaches E flat (316), which goes into the minor (320). No one in his right mind would regard this as a homecoming, and only those possessing 'absolute pitch' will even recognise the key as E flat. But we have reached the point when it is going to be necessary to plant the tonic in the ear – and so in comes Ex. 15 in E flat minor (322). The fact that this theme is so strikingly new makes it especially memorable: it is new, it is beautiful, it first appeared in the magical atmosphere of a foreign key. Therefore another appearance of it will also be arresting. Although we do not realise it, its key is now the tonic minor. By the time Beethoven reaches bar 338 he can emphasise the home dominant in such a way that we have the inescapable feeling that we are coming into the straight, and the strength of the return (still as far away as 398 and to be approached through some of the most exciting mystifications in the whole of music) is made absolute. To test and demonstrate this strength Beethoven makes the astounding self-cancelling modulations into F (408) and D flat (416) before surging back into a magnificently grounded tonic (430). Without the new theme in E minor at 284 all this would be impossible, and its reappearance in E flat minor at 322 is a piece of 'subliminal' advertising of the tonic so subtle as to render the most sly efforts of the modern Public Relations Officer no better than bellowing through a megaphone.

The *Eroica* needs a book to itself, so we must be content with a few more fugitive comments. In contrast to the first movement, the funeral march shows the kind of bigness that comes from slowness; the main theme itself is vast, and when its figures are broken into for the purposes of development their transformations are made even broader. (See how the phrase in bars 5 and 6 becomes that in the fugato beginning at 114, which is also retrospectively connected with the bass in the C major episode – rising quavers, from bar 69; thus are the two immensely different episodes in this colossal slow rondo connected.) The inscrutability of the deeper creative levels is illustrated by the early sketches of the scherzo – they are marked *tempo di minuetto*; this at least suggests that the *prestissimo* performances we often hear are too fast – the tempo, though quick, should allow the quavers in bar 9 and wherever they occur to be perfectly distinct. The second horn part in the trio is impossible at some of the speeds too often adopted, and to play the trio at a slower pace than the scherzo is a debased solution of the problem. The finale, on a bass and theme (in that order) from *Prometheus*, anticipates that of the Ninth Symphony in being neither variations nor sonata, nor even rondo, using elements of all three for its organic growth into a purely individual structure. The variation elements are impelled to expand into development, and periodic incursions of comparatively regular variations have a rondo-like effect. The elation eventually prompts the music to broaden its stride into a *poco andante*, and this inspired stroke has often been romantically misconstrued as a continuation of the funeral march into Heaven. Grove says, 'The March may well represent the death of the hero, and the interment of his mortal part. The *poco andante* is his flight to the skies.' This reads more like a prophecy of *Ein Heldenleben* than a description of the *Eroica* as I understand it. Beethoven's conception of a hero is not a romantic one; he is expressing the truth about human potential as he sensed it in himself. Napoleon is left far behind. The *andante* is no vision of Paradise — why, if it is, the powerful human stress, the intensely human doubt, even fear, that creeps across the music before the final *presto* breaks out like a last wave of heroic determination? There should be no need for heroism even in Valhalla, let alone Heaven. No — the meaning of these last grand paragraphs is surely this, that the hero, having experienced struggle, tragedy, joy, and awareness of power, surveys the past with a just and mounting sense of dignity. There is even a forgivable note of self-satisfaction in bars 392–5. Then comes the culminating and chastening realisation; he can never be without cause both to fear and to fight. Indomitably he faces the truth and the symphony ends with a blaze of defiance. Beethoven is the objective realist even when, as here, he is undoubtedly painting a self-portrait.

Symphony No. 4, in B Flat Major

The paucity of sketches for the Fourth Symphony has given rise to the supposition that it is entirely spontaneous; certainly the work is so felicitous as to suggest having been done at a sitting. Yet the symphony is by no means entirely sunny. We have already noted the deep mystery and tension of its slow introduction and its probable influence on the dark link between the last two movements of the Fifth. Critical reactions to the first performance of No. 4 found it crude and wayward, overcrowded with detail, lacking 'dignified simplicity'. Later comment went to the other extreme, culminating in Schumann's famous simile: 'like a slender Greek maiden between two Norse giants'. Neither view is right, though it is a compliment to the range and subtlety of Beethoven that both are understandable in context. There is decidedly no trace of crudity or want of dignity in this wonderfully balanced, richly executed score. But its grace is neither maidenly nor Greek; it is that of a giant who performs relaxed athletic movements with gigantic ease and fluency. There are muscles of steel beneath the silken skin of Beethoven's creature; sometimes they tense and flex with sudden force, though there is rarely more than a hint of irascibility. In the *adagio* there is deep tenderness, even passion, of a peculiarly masculine kind to which Schumann's image is scarcely apt, and its inner contrast between a pervasively rigid rhythm and the most gloriously free melodic invention Beethoven had yet achieved creates a unique fascination, a sublime discomfort of mind and senses.

Those who found the work crude and strange may well have been completely puzzled by this and by the dark pall of the introduction; such listeners, though their impressions were distorted, were right in not ignoring them, for the symphony is nowadays too often described as purely joyous. Joy it expresses in abundance, but its point surely is that light is no longer light when darkness is inconceivable; so the music emerges from an impenetrable blackness into gleaming sunlight whose vividness is thereafter constantly preserved by passing patches of cloud. The light is never again obscured but it is sometimes dimmed, as in the development of the first movement, some passages in the *adagio*, and in momentary gusty threats in the otherwise irrepressibly gay finale. It always shines out again, brighter than ever. This is as much a drama as the heroics of the Third and Fifth symphonies, albeit of a more elusive kind; to appreciate it is not to indulge in mystery-mongering, but to feel the richness and limitless sensitivity of the composer's mind.

Whether or not the Fourth was composed in one continuous burst, it abounds in subtleties no less than any other work of Beethoven known to have been more laboriously achieved. Basil Lam has made the point[1] that the treatment of the timpani is of consummate genius and that Beethoven was the first composer to take advantage of the fact that these instruments cannot be truly enharmonic. If the key is B flat, and the drum plays B flat, we know that this note is always B flat, even when the other instruments are playing A sharp in the dominant of B major. The entry of the drum in this situation, in a hushed pianissimo just before the reprise in the first movement, is a profound stroke that remained unique to Beethoven until Bruckner did something similar in his Sixth Symphony,[2] and it is such perfect strategy that it enables Beethoven to restore the tonic B flat without dominant preparation. The effect is, moreover, greatly enhanced by the fact that the timpani have hitherto played only one unobtrusive *p* note, and that an F – all its other entries have been *f* or *ff*. Not even in the mysterious quiet introduction has it been given anything to do until the *ff* at bar 36, despite the temptation Beethoven must have felt to out-rumble Haydn's *Drum-roll* Symphony. But his artistic vision is such that it is certain to have been the long view that decided this rather than any desire to avoid obvious comparison with Haydn.

We can perhaps get some idea of why Beethoven's contemporaries were baffled if we compare the introduction to No. 4 with superficially analogous ones by Haydn. Listeners of the day were quite used to the idea of a mysterious slow introduction leading to a gay *allegro*; Haydn had given them several examples with which they had become completely familiar. Take, for instance, the one already mentioned, the opening of his No. 103, in E flat (the *Drum-roll*). The atmosphere of mystery is conjured at the very start by the roll of the drum; it is increased by the fact that the ensuing melody in the lower instruments is unharmonised, and by its curious extension into six-bar phrases, ending in harmonised cadences. Here is the first of these:

Ex. 16

1   'Beethoven' in *The Symphony,* Vol. I (Pelican, 1966).
2   I have described this in *The Essence of Bruckner* (Gollancz, 1967).

There are no strange harmonies or modulations, nor is the key even minor. The last phrase of the melody grows into quiet harmonies that slowly drift to the dominant of C minor, where there is a pause. Here is the real mystery, to be contradicted by the lively E flat major beginning of the *allegro con spirito*. We should note especially that the continuity of Haydn's introduction is secured by plain melodic means, the mystery being in the slowness and instrumentation of its unfolding; the regular punctuation of related cadences provides clear footholds for the listener. Or examine the introduction to Haydn's previous symphony, No. 102, in B flat; instead of the drum-roll we have a unison tonic pause, followed by a regular four-bar phrase of harmonised melody:

Ex. 17

Then there is another pause, and another balancing four-bar phrase. After this come remarkable shifting modulations of the kind we have come to call Beethovenian, and these eventually settle on the home dominant in straightforward preparation for the *allegro vivace*. These strange harmonic shifts and the shortening of the phrase-lengths are heard against the background of regularity established by the opening; their mystery is like that of an intriguing picture placed on a wall the size of which is clearly seen.

Now consider Beethoven's introduction. It opens, like both of Haydn's, with a sustained note. This note, however, is held while a tonally ambiguous shape creeps under it on the strings:

Ex. 18

By the beginning of the sixth bar we realise that the opening note was a tonic pedal and that we have momentarily broken off at a strange kind of half-cadence. The music seems to wander about on (presumably) the home dominant, with weirdly detached notes and chords; then the sense of a home dominant is confirmed by the reappearance of the opening B flat (bar 13). Not till now can we be sure that the key of B flat is secure.

Nor can we realise until the creeping string phrase comes back in bar 14 that the opening B flat was not, as in Haydn, an unmeasured pause, but a gigantically slow upbeat. The return of the string phrase in bar 14 gives us a glimmer of an idea that some kind of pattern is forming. But it is a pattern on a vast scale, much too vast for the average hearer of Beethoven's time. Now the music, instead of making its strange (but this time expected) half-cadence, hangs on to the G flat that originally dropped to F (compare bars 6 and 18), and treats it as F sharp, so shifting the continuation on to the dominant of B:

Ex. 19

A long time afterwards, in the middle of the development, we again enter this magical region, where the drum executes the extraordinary stroke already mentioned; but we can know nothing of that now, as the detached abstracted chords lead us to expect a long sustained B in place of the original B flat. We get the B (bar 25), but it is treated as the third of a chord of G, now as an enormous quiet upbeat to a process in which, for the first time, harmonies begin to change at a rate approaching normality, creating a more easily assimilable harmonic rhythm (during this, in bar 29, we hear the only B flat chord in the introduction, but as a flat sixth in D minor). We begin to feel a firmer sense of direction as the music settles on the dominant of D minor with positively singable phrases:

Ex. 20

Repeated As rise in a tense crescendo. Then they are magnificently underpinned by dominant seventh chords, with the first entry of the drum on F. Now we can see why Beethoven has not hitherto used the timpani: the classical use of these instruments had always been to emphasise tonic and dominant, and Beethoven's art is deeply conditioned by the habits of his forebears and contemporaries, so he sees no reason why he should not take full advantage of these habits and make a new and startlingly reassuring use of the drum on what is now a dominant of devastating obviousness. There is another subtlety as he sweeps into the *allegro vivace*: the three slow *fortissimo* bars before the change of tempo confirm that the first four bars of the *allegro* itself are a mighty subdivided upbeat, corresponding to the sustained one at the beginning of the symphony. No wonder this introduction caused such dismay and confusion – its time-scale could not be perceived even in retrospect by those who took the ensuing *allegro* to be a rather heavy-handed imitation of Haydn.

In the *allegro vivace* the main theme proves capable of behaving both as a lively and characteristic idea in itself and as a neutral accompaniment; this enables Beethoven to create a very wide range of texture in this not very long movement. Typical of the tight rhythmic organisation is the way the syncopations beginning at bar 95 grow naturally from the fragment of the main theme being treated immediately before, where there is an implied accent on the second beat:

Ex. 21

The movement has a notable tendency to avoid the home subdominant (E flat); in the middle of the development (233) this key is touched, but it does not sound remotely like a subdominant and soon the music slips into utterly alien areas in preparation for the magical return and the stroke of genius with the drum. One reason for this eschewing of the subdominant (as such) is that the key of the *adagio* is going to be E flat; another is that in escaping from the darkness of the introduction the *allegro* strives to emphasise the tonic major and its even brighter dominant. In the first 89 bars only a few are without an insistent B flat somewhere, and this also has its long-term effect on the manner of the reprise, which the drum the more inevitably anticipates by injecting its soft B flat into an alien atmosphere. And the reprise itself is driven home without dominant preparation, so firmly grounded is B flat from the beginning of the *allegro*; the recapitulation begins at 337, with tonic instead of dominant preparation, and the long-delayed dominant confirmation is not properly delivered until the return of the syncopated transition at 369. So the function of the transition in the recapitulation is changed more subtly than usual; originally it was dominant preparation for F major and the second group – now it is dominant confirmation of B flat and the preceding first group. All this may seem boring to read about, but hear it truly and see if it is not a miracle. Observe finally in this movement how Beethoven stretches the last tutti (491) into 5+3 bars, leaving a final upbeat bar unspoken, to remind us quietly that both introduction and *allegro* began with upbeat periods. Schumann, with his addiction to regular phrasing, did not understand this, and 'corrected' Beethoven's five-bar period by cutting out one bar, the passage then becoming 6 bars plus one strong beat to end the piece.

The Fourth might also be called the Upbeat Symphony. Discussion of rhythmic structure (as opposed to enjoying the thing itself) is bound to read somewhat tediously – yet how much more meaningful is the opening of the *adagio* when we wake up to the fact that its first sentence begins in the second bar! Here is the correct phrasing:

Ex. 22

The first bar, giving out the characteristic rhythm, is a huge upbeat, like the first bar of the whole symphony. It is illuminating to go through the whole movement only to find that every time this bar recurs the situation is the same – except for two remarkable instances. The decorated versions of it at bars 17, 19, 72 and 74 are all upbeats, and Beethoven shows a powerful consistency in his approach to the first return of the beautiful main theme:

Ex. 23

'But,' says Beethoven, 'you thought that one bar at the beginning was self-sufficient, didn't you? – Very well then, I won't entirely disappoint you.' So he chooses the most miraculous way of pleasing our first natural instinct. The movement is a spacious rondo; after the first return of the main theme (bar 43) the music goes with majestic passion into E flat minor (50), whence it subsides poetically on to the dominant of G flat (54). The violins weave delicate arabesques, stretching them into a six-bar period. Then the harmony falls softly into the expected G flat major (60) – where the bassoon shyly plays the opening rhythm, *pianissimo*. The exquisite paradox lies in the fact that while this is the quietest and most mysterious statement of the rhythm so far, it is also the only one in the whole movement in which it stands rhythmically alone, as a one-bar period. It is also for the first time a downbeat (remember we are referring to the larger 'beat' of the period, not the internal beat of the bar – though at this point period and bar become the same length, as the quotation shows):

Ex. 24

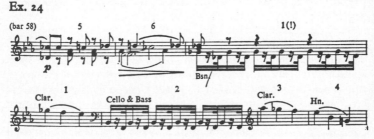

As can be seen in Ex. 24 the rhythm then reverts to its customary weak-beat function (bars 62 and 64). Such is Beethoven's way of keeping the music in the air; almost any other composer would have laboured the obvious by using the rhythm to mark the heavy beginnings of the music's periods, with earthbound result. Because of this subtlety Beethoven can allow the music to move almost entirely in simple four-bar periods (even the marvellous, seemingly extempore second theme at 26 and 81, one of the most wonderful things ever given to the clarinet). Just before the end of the movement we hear the rhythm for the last time, remote on the *pianissimo* drum, but for the first and only time on the strong beat of a larger period and with (subtlety of subtleties) a quaver rest in place of its first pulse. One longs to be able to describe these things in the poetry they deserve, instead of in bald jargon, but they are themselves untranslatable poetry. One can only hint at some of the things that make Beethoven what he is; these are the details that give inner life to an art, whether or not the listener understands or even observes them.

In a sense the Fourth Symphony is a study in subtlety of movement such as aptly expresses delight. It is many other things besides, but there is something curiously fascinating in the way the scherzo, after the vast concealed syncopation of the period-structure of the *adagio*, takes obvious pleasure in the deliberate disruption of smaller-scaled rhythms. The larger periods are all regular fours with interspersed sixes, but their *enchaînement* is unusual – five four-bar periods before the double bar, and a delightful stretching effect up to the return of the theme at bar 53 (4+4+6 and 4+4+4+6), all enlivened in the most deliciously contradictory manner by cross-rhythms and rapid modulations, like fish darting towards a morsel of bread, their erratic movements contained and carried by a firm current (the sustained line in bassoons and cellos from 35 onwards). The trio by contrast spreads itself with grand regularity; it is often played too slowly – the marking is *un poco meno allegro*, which does not mean the rheumatic *andantino* we frequently hear, making the second repetition intolerable. This is the first of Beethoven's scherzos that brings in its trio twice; anyone who is impatient with this device misses the point: Beethoven is not merely filling up the space allowed him by the quicker speed of a scherzo as opposed to a minuet. It is all a matter of momentum: if the music is properly played we should feel that the second appearance of the trio has come spinning round before it can be halted, and the rotation could go on until Beethoven, like a *deus ex machina*, chooses to stop it. A conductor who wants to cut the repeat is unable to give a good performance, for he cannot feel what is essential to the movement. We must, of course, insist that this is a scherzo, despite Beethoven's tongue-in-cheek use of the term 'minuet'; he cannot have meant it to be even as slow as Haydn's quickest minuets, for his original marking was *allegro molto e vivace* (the *molto* afterwards crossed out). He may well have been thinking of Haydn's wish that someone would show him how to write a new kind of minuet. This movement, incidentally, starts like the first two with an upbeat – not the little upbeat crotchet at the beginning, but the whole first four bars, which make an upbeat period; the joke does not become apparent until we reach the double bar. Beethoven's final prank is more violent; there is an extra phrase in which, as Schumann says, 'the horns have one more question to put'. The question is as unanswerable as 'If God is omnipotent, could He make a weight so heavy that He couldn't lift it?', for it is 'Does this sound right because it's wrong or wrong because it's right?' It is meant to sound gloriously wrong, and with perfect rightness.

Like the scherzo the effervescent finale starts with a four-bar upbeat period, the first strong period beginning deceptively with the *p* in the fifth bar and opening a regular set of periods (4+4+6+6) leading to the first sustained tutti at bar 21. The stretching of the two six-bar periods creates a tension that makes the first twenty bars feel like a giant upbeat, containing a number of fascinating ambiguities. As with most of Beethoven's repeats, that of the exposition is necessary for reasons of rhythm as well as of proportion. This movement contains as many rhythmic ingenuities as the rest of the symphony, though its directness and its character of a *moto perpetuo* tend to deceive the ear into supposing it to be simpler than it is. The *moto perpetuo* aspect often leads conductors into excessive speed, which destroys its natural grace, breadth, and even leisure. The metronome mark is further evidence of Beethoven's metronome having been faulty: $\downarrow$ =80 is a tempo not even a string orchestra of Heifetzes could be sure of maintaining safely (to say nothing of the wretched clarinet and bassoon players), yet the indication is *allegro ma non troppo*. A reasonable pace would seem to me to be around $\downarrow$ =116.

Symphony No. 5, in C Minor

It would be a waste of space to describe the most familiar of all symphonies in the usual terms. But this is perhaps a suitable place to discuss the shape of the Fifth as Beethoven first conceived it (at least the form in which it was first played); it has rarely been given thus, and there is a good case for so recording it. At the first performance in 1808 (and some subsequent ones) the work was done with scherzo and trio repeated: i.e., scherzo, trio, scherzo, trio – then the final shortened pianissimo restatement of the scherzo that both leads to and reappears (altered) in the finale. Beethoven had already made such a double repeat in the Fourth Symphony (the Sixth, too, which had its first performance with the Fifth, displayed this feature), but soon after the first few airings of No. 5 he decided to cut out the repeat of scherzo and trio, as shown by a letter to Breitkopf and Härtel, dated 21 August 1810:

> I have found the following error still remaining in the Symphony in C minor; namely, in the third movement in 3/4 time, where the minor comes back after the major. I quote the bass part thus:

> The two bars which are crossed out are too many, and must be erased, of course, in all parts.

As is well known, this correction of Beethoven's was ignored until Mendelssohn drew the publishers' attention to it in 1846, receiving from them the explanation that 'according to the original manuscript, Beethoven had the intention, as in many other symphonies, to repeat the minor three times and the major twice. Hence in the manuscript the bars struck out in the letter are marked with "1" and the two following with "2". This, as well as the remark written above in red pencil "Si replica con Trio allora" was overlooked in printing.' I once erroneously stated that no score of this symphony was published during Beethoven's lifetime;[1] an octavo score was in fact issued by Breitkopf and Härtel in March 1826 – something I had known for years but unaccountably forgotten. This score still contains the two 'redundant' bars, and it caused confusion and controversy for a long time; eminent musicians (among them Berlioz) often tried to find musical excuses for retaining the two extra bars. One cannot help wondering how closely (if at all) the

1 Article in *The Score* (January 1960).

34

composer supervised the publication of this first edition of the score; that he did not reiterate his complaint of 1810 is, to say the least, extraordinary. It is always possible that ill-health and his preoccupation with the last quartets made him disinclined to bother with the Fifth Symphony, and – I think – not impossible that he never finally made up his mind about the matter. Perhaps by 1826 the subject was too remote to claim his full attention. Whatever the truth about that, the manuscript creates still more doubt.

On the autograph there are a number of illegible instructions in his own scrawl (written in both pencil and ink, which suggests they were put there at different, indeterminable, times), the incomprehensibility of which is made worse by the fact that the passage occurs at the end of a right-hand page and the instructions spill over to the next page. But the '1' and '2' and the '*Si replica con Trio allora*' are not crossed out. These uncertainties, together with the fact that Beethoven's letter to Breitkopf was written less than two years after the first performance (at a time when he still had seventeen years of life left in which to think about the symphony, during which period he could at any time have altered the autograph had he so wished), make it not unreasonable to reconsider the whole question with an open mind. The documentary facts being both indecisive and contradictory, we are faced with a purely artistic problem of a supremely exciting kind, one that can eventually be solved only by a consensus of thoughtful and imaginative (and above all respectful) opinion. Therefore it concerns the ordinary listener more than the fact-finding scholar.

We have already noted that the question of repeats is with Beethoven a profound matter, judged by him on many more levels than are open to the average performer. Leaving out of account the perennial impatience, lack of stamina (except in crescendos or accelerandos), or sheer hatred of music shown by a good many conductors, most of the thoughtful ones who know their Beethoven would instinctively agree to omit the big repeat in the finale of the Fifth Symphony. Why do the majority leave it out? Presumably because they intuitively feel that it upsets the proportions. They are right. The scherzo is over before it is properly established and is then annihilated by a blazing C major movement that proceeds to repeat the whole of its weighty first section. The return of the scherzo in the middle of the finale, moreover, is weakened by being reduced to the condition of a pathetic 'flashback' by all this crushingly disproportionate C major. But as soon as one realises that Beethoven's original conception included total repeat of scherzo and trio, the nature of and reason for the repeat in the finale become brightly illuminated.

The character of the scherzo is magnetic and obsessive. Even more than its companion movements in the Fourth, Sixth, and Seventh symphonies it seems to cry out for 'circular' repetition. If it is given thus it gains a fearsome momentum, as if nothing can stop its fateful stride. Beethoven has, moreover, shortened the scherzo on its final *pianissimo* appearance, an effect which can be fully appreciated only if the complete unleashed version has already twice confronted the hearer. The grimly persistent scherzo and wild trio have been crashed into the brain by repetition that hints at endlessness; at the point when yet another return of the scherzo in its original overpowering form would be unbearable Beethoven, with one of his greatest strokes of genius, makes the music disappear into a void, so that we are not certain whether it can still be heard at a vast distance or whether it is merely reverberating faintly in the brain. The fact that it is shortened enhances the impression of a vague disturbed memory; then it vanishes into nothing but the dim sensation of a remotely beating drum and a hushed drone, a scarcely perceptible distant activity. The sky is huge and black – but there comes a tiny point of light. As it expands with frightening speed and mounting energy, we do not know whether to hope or to fear – until the whole universe is abruptly ablaze. (It is a fact not often realised, so powerful is the conditioning of hindsight and familiarity, that there is nothing in this dark link passage to give an inkling of what is to follow it; but it is still possible, with the right kind of effort, to listen to it as Beethoven intended.) Now as the scherzo was insistently momentous in its grim self-repetition, so is the finale in its brilliance. It *must* repeat its exposition in order fully to counteract the effect of the obsessively repeated scherzo. Furthermore this repeat prolongs the blaze to such an extent that the previous movement is almost forgotten – but not quite. All at once the light fades. Once more the sky is black, and the mesmeric scherzo *is still going on*. The light returns and thereafter remains; but the impressiveness of the whole experience depends on the sense that the return of the scherzo in the heart of the finale is not a mere remembrance, a plaintive 'flashback', but a reality. *It is still there*. The finale is no romantic 'triumph'; the antithesis of scherzo and finale is an elemental phenomenon, and the finale has the last word only because it suggests a condition in which human power can thrive, not because the world of the scherzo has ceased to exist.

The repeat of the finale exposition is thus necessary in the light of the original conception of the scherzo, and the repeat of scherzo and trio creates a momentum that gives reality to a later reappearance that is otherwise little more than a fantastic whim. If scherzo and trio are not repeated, the repeat in the finale should not be observed. My feeling is that the proper thing to do is to restore Beethoven's first colossal idea despite his own apparent uncertainty. The 'final decisions' of the great masters (in so far as they are known) are often the subject of pious nonsense uttered by those to whom words are, as Alastair Sim perfectly said, 'the anodyne for the pain of thinking'; on the other hand it is also usually intrepid and insolent to meddle with great works of art. But in this case Beethoven's intentions are not absolutely clear and we can reach a solution only by using the kind of internal evidence that will tax our imagination and intuition. The experiment should be made many times, the symphony performed both ways, until the choice becomes obvious.

For me, the printed edition of the C minor Symphony is a mutilated makeshift; can we be sure that Beethoven might not in the end have returned to his first idea, as he restored the repeat in the first movement of the *Eroica*? Are we certain that he really agreed with his friends that the *Grosse Fuge* is not the proper climax to Op. 130? Can we dogmatise and say that his last version of *Fidelio* is absolutely final, that if the occasion had arisen he might not have brought back the psychologically profound music he first wrote for the moment of Florestan's rescue, excised in favour of some flat spoken dialogue? Judgement must remain on the artistic level in all these cases, for in none of them is there documentary evidence to prove beyond doubt what Beethoven thought at various times, or whether or how often he changed his mind. The Fifth Symphony with repeated scherzo and trio and the repeat in the finale will raise new interpretative problems for any conductor attempting it; if he finds no other profit in the exercise he will at least have been made to discover the music afresh. Sir Adrian Boult once pointed out to me that a serious difficulty in observing the finale repeat is to avoid a sense of anticlimax with each return of the main theme. But he himself convincingly demonstrated how with a skilful reservation of power each appearance of the theme can be increased in intensity.

In these days of thematic analysis that disregards all other aspects of music, characteristic of a period in which the lack of genuine invention has caused a fixation upon mere lifeless materials, we should be wary of the first movement of Beethoven's Fifth. Tovey exploded a long time ago the idea that the whole piece was derived from its famous first four notes; at the same time he dealt faithfully with the fallacy that there is a connection between these and certain other rhythms in the other movements. If Beethoven had wanted us to feel a real connection between

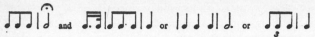

he would have made the derivation explicit or (if subtle) organic. For all I know, some musical Strabismus has already found a deeply significant connection between the main theme of the finale and the first flute part in bars 10–15 of the slow movement; if so he is welcome to the priority, but it is bad luck for him that the violins do not make the answer as follows, subtly changing the accent of the triplet (which is itself, of course, derived from the opening of the symphony):

Ex. 25

If we want to find genuinely organic thematic work we should not normally expect much success in finding cross-connections between Beethoven's separate movements; we should listen to (not look at) what happens inside a single movement. The power of the first movement, for instance, depends as much on what is *not* developed from the initial figure as on what is. Haydn is inclined, much more than Beethoven, to base whole movements on single figures or rhythms (the first movement of Symphony No. 28, in A major, or the last of No. 103, in E flat, for instance), and this tends to restrict the scale of the designs. The first movement of Beethoven's C minor symphony opens out vast spaces that might seem to be out of context but are observed from within tightly drawn boundaries. The horn call (derived from the opening) that introduces the second group at bar 59 itself anticipates organically the theme that follows it:

Ex. 26

and the way in which Beethoven expands this material in the coda (398 onwards) is astounding in its organic inevitability and, above all, in its freedom. Here we find a mighty, extended passage where the 'pervasive' rhythm is entirely absent. Notice also how the first half of the stormy development is not based on (*a*) but on (*b*):

Ex. 27

and its inversion, while the second half is largely powered by Ex. 26 (*b*) without its three quavers. This is what classical composition is all about.

The dramatic nature of the Fifth Symphony has ensured its frequent maltreatment by the type of romantic conductor who is the equivalent of the ham actor. Beware of the fool who knocks out the opening bars in a slow tempo, then tears off like a maniac from bar 6; we may be sure that he will perform the same maddening trick at every similar point, in order to demonstrate two things (a) his lion-tamer-like control of the orchestra, and (b) (unconscious) that he has no idea of the tempo. There is, in fact, a magnificently cogent tempo in which every quaver is like a hammer – the pace must be of incorruptible steadiness, halted only by those mighty pauses that mean nothing without a proper pulse to measure them by. Mahler once gave some sound advice to a young conductor: 'If you think you are boring your audience, go slower, not faster.'

Symphony No. 6, in F Major (Pastoral)

Beethoven once dismissed an overture by Weber as 'nothing but a string of diminished sevenths' – to which it has been retorted that Beethoven himself was rather fond of diminished sevenths. It is true that he made more striking use of them than any other previous composer and that they may be found in most of his works, often at crucial moments. But his use of the chord is always structural in terms of sonata drama, not merely atmospheric or as a convenient lever into a remote key. This chord is so easily treated enharmonically and so productive of facile mystery that it became the curse of many an early romantic composer. No one knew its real power better than Beethoven, and consequently no composer has shown a finer instinct in not using it. The late Julius Harrison, whose luminous conversation I sorely miss, once pointed out to me that there is not a single diminished seventh in the Pastoral Symphony until the storm. In the first movement of No. 5 they are legion; yet even in that tense symphony we find Beethoven avoiding the chord at the very point where Weber (had he thought of such an idea at all) might have seized upon it – early in the dramatic link between the last two movements. But Beethoven knew that the darkness, softness, and the continuing ambiguous A flat in the bass are far more gripping than any diminished seventh harmony, which in this work could by this time have little surprise value – until the bass slips down through G to F sharp, now revealed as leading note to a dominant pedal. But in the Sixth the simplest diatonic harmony reigns throughout the first three movements, with hardly a suspicion of chromaticism even in the searching modulations of the slow movement. Nevertheless in sheer richness, variety, and transparency of sound this symphony is surely the most wonderful score Beethoven ever committed to paper.

Beethoven's imaginative treatment of the orchestra is unprecedented even in his own work, and became a mine for later composers, notably Berlioz, whose orchestration would often be inconceivable without Beethoven's example. It is time we acknowledged that when all the splendours and ingenuities of the nineteenth-century orchestra and its best exponents have been given their due, Beethoven remains one of the greatest masters of orchestration. No later composer has surpassed (or, I would say, even equalled) the poetry of the 'Scene by the brook', and certainly no one but Beethoven himself has achieved anything like it with such limited means, instrumental or harmonic. Nor can the most enormous apparatus in the hands of later composers rival the sublimity of Beethoven's storm, in which the classical orchestra is augmented by only one piccolo and two (not three) trombones. With Beethoven the music and the scoring are one; all elements in the work are interdependent. Rimsky-Korsakov's dictum that good orchestration is good counterpoint needs no more perfect illustration than the Pastoral Symphony. Superficially this may seem a strange proposition, obvious as it is that this is the least overtly contrapuntal of all the Beethoven symphonies; yet time after time the ear is attracted by some exquisite felicity of scoring, only to realise that it is essentially a matter of polyphony.

Of all the movements the first is the most consistently harmonic rather than linear in feeling; yet paradoxically it is, apart from the scherzo, harmonically the simplest part of the work. Despite its concentration on the vertical or harmonic aspect of the sound, its use of harmony (or rather, the harmony it uses) is almost primitive – there is little else but triads and sevenths. But it is because of this that the tonal breadth and range of the movement can be so clearly perceived. This restraint is the other face of its astonishing thematic repetitiousness; the immense tonal range is explored with so perfect a sense of proportion that the long stretches of simple chords and little figures that repeat themselves like leaves on a tree create a sublime monotony that has caused delight and wonderment for a century and a half. Grove says, 'When the sameness of fields, woods, and streams can become distasteful, then will the Pastoral Symphony weary its hearers'. Such an achievement comes as surely from strength as the most violent action; to do it Beethoven needed ample reserves of energy, for the most relaxed of pleasures become penances when we are too exhausted even for them. The deeper the reserves, the better the physical and mental health, the fuller the capacity for happiness and the greater the power of relaxation. This is the lesson of the Sixth Symphony, the Violin Concerto, the Fourth Piano Concerto, and many other Beethoven masterpieces.

The simple textures of the first movement are offset by the proliferation of the *andante molto mosso*, elaborate in detail as it is expansive and leisurely, a complete sonata organism that finds time even to stand still. The first movement not only eschewed chromatic harmony, but contained not one chromatic appoggiatura, and those diatonic ones it did produce were unobtrusive. The undulating movement of the 'Scene by the brook' produces appoggiaturas by the dozen, but again none of them is chromatic; they are, however, a prominent feature of the piece and give it much of its characteristic expression. The movement also shows another sympathetic reaction from the *allegro ma non troppo*, whose simple diatonicism and deliberate monotony made the key of F major, in the recapitulation and coda, as seemingly inescapable as green in the country. Now Beethoven knows the exact frontier between poetic monotony and tedium. He wants the key of the slow movement to be B flat major; he also intends it to be in full sonata form, with a long and wonderfully lazy second group in the dominant, which will be F major. The danger is clear – if the music falls into a long stretch of plain F major too soon after the first movement there could be more than a threat of tedium. So Beethoven stays as long as possible in B flat, allowing the long and beautiful main theme to unfold twice, even bringing it to a full close at bar 18. With remarkable nerve he then stops in B flat with what would seem to be a new (transition?) theme if it were more than a few stray thoughts. (We stand still, forgetting the motion of the stream, lost in a brown study.) Now we continue, and as if nothing had happened the brook (and the main theme) claims our attention once more, *still in B flat*. This time the harmony unhurriedly drifts towards the dominant and in another six and a half.bars (the bars are long in this piece) we are in F major and the real second group begins (bar 27).

The breadth of the first subject is amazing enough, but the treatment of the second group is even more bold. Now is the time to beware of the too solid establishment of F major, in view of its effect in the first movement, and the genius of Beethoven's solution lies in the extreme rarity of root chords of F in this long passage; most of it is over a pedal C, and only near the end of it do we find an F root in the bass occurring at the beginning of a downbeat period. (Those, for instance, at bars 30 and 32 begin the second halves of two-bar periods.) And the masterly evasion of the full close by turning into submediant harmony and a new theme at bar 33, thus keeping the music gloriously floating, is as structurally perceptive as it is magnificently poetic. By such wonderful means is the danger set by F major circumvented, and to such purpose that at the end of the exposition Beethoven is able to rest in F major (50–56) with the same indolent comfort as in B flat. Throughout the development, which shares with that of the first movement a predilection for long stretches at a time in one harmonic region, the scoring and the modulations are miraculous, conveying a depth of sound that suggests visual perspective. The imagination is so sensitively precise that the sounds of nature seem to be coming from different distances; the superb changes from G major to E flat and thence to G flat, C flat, and the home dominant, accompanied by constantly varying orchestration of astounding beauty, seem to change the direction in which we are facing without moving us from the enchanted spot.

The rest of the work has already been mentioned in terms of its relation to the corresponding part of the Fifth Symphony (p. 40); a few brief points must now suffice. Beethoven is still concerned to prevent F major from becoming earthbound and near the opening of the scherzo he takes full note of a hint he had already given himself in the F major Bagatelle of Op. 33 – a delicious turn to a bright D major for the second phrase:

Ex. 28

The affectionate humour with which he parodies a village band has been often commented upon; but we should note that this scherzo, like its companions in the Fourth and Seventh symphonies and the original version of the Fifth (as well as in a number of chamber works), has a double repetition. The trio, incidentally, begins (I think) not with the change to 2/4 time but with the oboe theme at bar 91. Beethoven confirms this by his truncation of the last return of the scherzo. With the storm we hear the immense effect of the long-denied diminished seventh; how magical are bars 9 and 10! And another amazing fact – the colossal *fortissimo* outbreak at bar 21 is the only chord of F minor in the whole symphony. Beethoven's storm is not, like Sibelius's in his music for *The Tempest*, the naked inhuman elements. It is a storm experienced, a challenge to the human observer, in whom it arouses a powerful response; notice how the bass *sings* as it sweeps in great descending phrases. It is this human core in the music that makes possible the joyful expansive relaxation of the finale. The storm produces in the man pent feelings and energies that at length flow widely and sweetly in a vivid but calm affirmation of life. With the finale Beethoven returns to the chaste harmonic restraint of the rest of the symphony; but the freedom of the storm is not entirely given up, and he allows himself the luxury of one solitary German sixth (bar 93).

Symphony No. 7, in A Major

The Ninth would not have been possible without both the Seventh and Eighth symphonies, and I hope it will emerge from what follows that Beethoven is now moving into a different stride. Of all the symphonies, the Fourth and Seventh are perhaps the most difficult to describe. Those aspects of No. 4 that relate it to other works ease interestingly the writer's task. No. 7 can, as we shall see, be very interestingly related to No. 8, but in all other respects there is about it something almost threateningly aloof, mysteriously indescribable, that should give pause to the most garrulous commentator. Tovey made two pertinent remarks about it: 'The symphony is so overwhelmingly convincing and so obviously untranslatable, that it has for many years been treated quite reasonably as a piece of music, instead of as an excuse for discussing the French Revolution' . . . 'The trio will always remain as marvellous as ever, though we may not be able to remember a time when we did not know it by heart.' To originate the obvious must be an artist's greatest hope, and the reasons why this trio sounds marvellous are to do with Beethoven's new treatment of tonality in this extraordinary symphony; they are not in any way connected with the nature of the subject-matter itself. Most listeners are now so familiar with the Seventh Symphony that few stop to consider how 'obvious' some of its strokes are. How many notice the number of simple scale passages it contains, or those things that would clearly belong to it alone only if someone else tried to reproduce them? The material is itself largely of such primitive simplicity as to be part of some basic impersonal vocabulary. This work contains more apparent formulae than any other except the first two of Beethoven's symphonies, yet its individuality is such as to mesmerise the listener. The secret cannot be in the formulae themselves; it is in the context, the current in which they float. This aspect of the music is anything but conventional (or simple) and is determined by a wonderful new approach to tonality. Beethoven here colours the whole work with an uncomplicated but hitherto entirely unfamiliar attitude to keys; the main key is A major, but as well as allowing the music to explore normally related tonalities he makes startlingly systematic use of the foreign keys of C major and F major. The indefinable character of the whole symphony is determined by Beethoven's enormously powerful imagination in tackling this situation.

The colossal introduction is based on the plainest raw material: scales, slow turns, dotted rhythms, repeated notes, simple minims striding in deliberate chord formations. It would appear merely formal if one examined only its thematic invention. Take the following fragments, for instance:

Ex. 29

It is the treatment of tonality allied to a vast rhythmic sense that generates the magic, as compelling as the most inspired and gigantic architecture. Having established the main key (A major) with the utmost firmness at the outset, Beethoven, with unprecedented spaciousness, moves far afield; he does not take the usual course of opening out towards the dominant (which in this introduction is used only as an extended chord of preparation, not as a key), but instead swings deliberately into the depths of C major and a new, formally measured, woodwind theme (Ex. 29 (*c*)) that is nothing in itself but which, by its very simplicity, allows the hearer's imagination to be captured by the atmosphere (i.e. the tonality) in which it is discovered. This C major seems deep and remote, especially heard so early. Yet, as if there were nothing remarkable about it, Beethoven moves spaciously back towards the home key, and another great tutti intervenes, apparently bent on this object, and moving with incorruptible deliberation. But as the first tutti subsided into C major, this one goes into F major, an area of even deeper shadow relative to A major. The woodwind theme reappears in a profounder atmosphere than before. The immense and simple but disturbingly impressive changes of tonality, theme, and dynamics give the whole a sense of incalculable dimensions such as had never been approached in music before, and which renders the Seventh Symphony still unique.

This is no more than a beginning, and the two alien keys permeate not only the introduction but the whole symphony, which seems continually to be translating itself from dimension to dimension. The three tonal protagonists, A, C, and F, seem more like dimensions than keys; the composer's genius is able unfalteringly to devise the perfect means, at any moment, of preserving the astonishing effect. When the music goes into C or F we invariably have the impression that these are two remote but strangely related worlds; our home planet (A) revolves round the sun, but C and F exist in another part of space altogether, companions of some other star in some other galaxy. Music in this symphony has become multidimensional.

There are other implications, one especially striking. Throughout the first three movements there is a process that strongly anticipates the so-called 'progressive tonality' of Nielsen. The second movement is in A minor, and to this mode of A the pair of alien keys, C and F, are much more easily related than to A major. This allows them to emerge less obtrusively but more expectedly – so much so that the scherzo breaks out with F as its main key. Now it is A major that is the foreigner; the very first clause of the scherzo makes a modulation to A with a staggering wrench:

Ex. 30

In this context A cannot sound like a key in its own right – only like the dominant of D, but always to be violently contradicted, except when the trio emerges in a resplendent D major:

Ex. 31

Again the marvellous effect of the music depends largely upon its key; the theme of the trio is in no way remarkable, but Beethoven has set it in so fascinating yet so inevitable a tonal atmosphere that it never fails. At least it should not, if it is played at the proper tempo, rather than the funereal pace with which most conductors paralyse themselves into an inability to make the repeats so clearly indicated by Beethoven, and so necessary to the momentum of the movement as a whole. The proper speed is as marked, *assai meno presto*; Beethoven has not dropped the *presto*.

After the scherzo has closed in F, only the most furious vehemence can reinstate A as the rightful tonic; so the stunning force of the finale has a purely musical function and is not merely a baseless outburst of noise. A major has to be rammed home by hammer blows on its dominant:

Ex. 32

The finale succeeds in making C and F sound as remote as they did at first, and this dramatic new use of tonality creates a limitless source of energy. But the whole is so schematic as to produce a deep-laid sense of something fundamentally static, a feeling of gigantic circular motion, accentuated by the key-structure, the system of repeats, and the unified concentration upon rhythm. The energy is somehow mysteriously contained. If all the repeats in the Seventh are played, the rhythmic insistence enhances the circular effect; it is a kind of paradox – at the same time as the listener is swept off his feet he is subtly impressed by a sense of unity so immutable as to be a static phenomenon. The big repeats in the first and last movements are designed to complete the effect. On p. 10 I noted the 'curious self-sufficiency' of the Seventh and Eighth Symphonies; it arises from this paradox in both cases, though the Eighth in some ways carries the matter further (which is perhaps why Beethoven, after some critics had compared it unfavourably with No. 7, growled, 'That's because it's so much better than the other').

Symphony No. 8, in F Major

If Beethoven had not called the Eighth his 'little one' would it have seemed to us so small? Certainly it is not long but, as we have seen, one of this composer's most amazing abilities is to expand his thought while contracting the physical dimensions of its form. The first impression, at the start of No. 8, is of something condensed, yet as the music grows we begin to perceive that it has been presented to us, as it were, end-on. It is as if we see a cigar first from one end, only afterwards realising that the shape is long. After the compact first theme, which is rather like the end-view of the cigar, the thing begins to stretch, as if the cigar were being turned before our eyes:

Ex. 33

And it turns out to be a magnificent cigar, the symphony as a whole. Its finale is one of Beethoven's most expansive creations, unprecedented in form, and one of the origins of new discoveries in the so-called 'third period'. We shall come to this, but meanwhile there are a few observations to be made about the other movements. The first shows how concentrated a sonata organism can be, and proves that the greatest variety is possible in a short space. We find this also in the Quartet in F minor, Op. 95, written a couple of years earlier; there the mood is dark, here it is powerfully humorous. Consider the essence of sonata. Because its simplest developed shape seems superficially to comprise three sections – exposition, development, and recapitulation (a coda is not always present) – some writers have described it as ternary. In fact it is binary. Since the first part ends in a new key the development (or, as the Germans much more precisely call it, the *Durchführung*, the leading-through part) is essentially a means of returning to the home key, often by devious routes, to the recapitulation, together with which it constitutes the true, balancing second part. The recapitulation itself attracts everything as if gravitationally, and however large the development it must never lose its fluidity, must never achieve real stability, until the moment of reprise. That in the first movement of the *Eroica*, vast though it is, is as much a link, or free flight between fixed points, as are the few bars in the *Figaro* overture. In the opening movement of the Eighth

Symphony Beethoven emphasises this function of the development by making its total effect that of a single vast crescendo, so that when we arrive at the reprise it is with a simple but thrilling sense of climax. A further, deeper, and more complex treatment of this idea will be found in the first movement of the Ninth. Here we find the straightest form of it, which has greatly influenced Sibelius, especially in the finale of his Second Symphony and the first movement of his Third. Nielsen also shows consistent mastery of the 'crescendo-type' development, though usually with a different purpose involving progressive tonality. Beethoven's sense of fulfilment at the climax of this particular development was so great that at first he was content to follow the recapitulation with the briefest of codas. He afterwards expanded it, and the passage between bars 333 and 361 is an afterthought.

There is another way in which the first movement of No. 8 is unusual. The common idea of sonata assumes that the exposition is the strictest, most business-like part, where discursiveness is not to be encouraged. The development (sometimes called by those contradictions in terms, the romantic pundits, the 'free fantasia') is supposed to be the place where anything goes. Beethoven here most decidedly reverses these impressions. While it is never possible to accuse him of music in which 'anything goes', it is in the exposition that we find the variety, humour, changes of mood and colour, while the development cuts its path as straight as a Roman road. This is a characteristic of Beethoven's last period, yet another indication of the prophetic nature of this enormous little symphony. The Eighth was at first dismissed as a reversion to an earlier manner, perhaps because the third movement is a minuet that follows a *scherzando*, as in the E flat Piano Sonata, Op. 31 no. 3. Beethoven's contemporaries could scarcely have foreseen such works as the B flat Quartet, Op. 130, where the use of short intermediate movements of great variety became a new feature heralding an expanding finale (the *Grosse Fuge* in the original form of the work); that very phenomenon is trenchantly anticipated by the Eighth Symphony, whose finale is also expansive. We can compare this symphony at every point with Op. 31 no. 3, which it superficially resembles, and see how, while both explore new possibilities, the Eighth looks much further beyond itself than the piano sonata.

This symphony is also foil and companion to the Seventh. Its key-structure is without resemblance to its predecessor's; its rhythmic organisation, no less concentrated, is not of the same kind. Nor has it an elaborate system of repeats: one in the first movement and the usual ones in the minuet. But what is explicit in the Seventh is in the Eighth implicit; what the A major symphony achieves by exhaustive methods the F major produces by suggestion and hint, becoming fully explicit only in its finale. The whole of No. 7 describes a great circle; No. 8 begins with a main theme that is itself a completed ring:

Ex. 34

No previous Beethoven symphony starts with a self-contained tune, and not even Mozart dared begin a symphony thus. (He often opened so in a concerto, and this is easily possible in a ritornello that is basically static and introductory.) It is significant that when Haydn began a symphonic first *allegro* with a clear-cut self-completing tune he usually took care to precede it by a slow introduction, as in his last symphony. Only a foolish young composer or a wise old one would have started as Beethoven does in the Eighth, a stroke possible only after the experience of No. 7; the opening of No. 8 is not just a short tune — it is a microcosm, the crystallisation of a sense of self-sufficiency, emerging from the total effect of the previous symphony. It is worth remembering that these two symphonies were separated only by months. After such a condensed beginning, Beethoven is free to expand, so the rest of the exposition is by contrast positively discursive, much space having been saved for it. The ensuing development accentuates the 'circular' idea by insisting upon the opening figure, which revolves upon itself with growing obsessiveness until the whole tune breaks out at the climax like the hum from a spinning top that has reached critical speed.

Whereas the Seventh insists on wholesale repeats (which lamentably we rarely hear in performances) the Eighth tends wittily to hint at and then deny them. The *allegretto scherzando* makes as if to go round and round, and its little coda is a gay gesture dismissing the obvious. The reaction from this could not possibly be a symphonic scherzo, and the exquisite and intricately fashioned polyphony of the minuet is a further means of strengthening the impression of self-containedness; this is a gentle unhurried reconnaissance across the borders of a later, not an earlier, style. The greatest advance, however, comes in the finale, as much a leap into a new world as the last paragraphs of the Second Symphony. Here is an absolutely fresh blend of sonata and rondo, never attempted before. A rondo, even when lively, is static in essence, 'circular' in movement. What has so far been an implicit recognition of the nature of No. 7 will now become explicit in this last movement, whose function it is to enlarge the scope of the work as a whole. This wonderful finale is at once a simple rondo and a very elaborate true sonata movement; there are two developments and two recapitulations. The first development begins at bar 91 and the first recapitulation at 161. Then (in what is usually and wrongly described as an enormous coda) comes a second development (267), another recapitulation (355) and a genuine coda (438). So each recapitulation serves as a rondo reprise. Beethoven later returned to this plan, with totally different effect; the first movement of the A minor Quartet, Op. 132, traces its own gloomy circle and gives rise to a sense of poignant endlessness, remote from the brilliance of this finale that strikes bright sparks as a sword from a rock. In the symphony the famous C sharp that bursts savagely into the soft F major theme makes so fierce a collision in the second recapitulation that the theme is hurled from its smooth F major road-surface on to a very rough field, whence it is scared back again by a herd of bulls (personified by brass and drums). One is reminded of the incident when Beethoven, walking (or rather stampeding) in the country and singing (or rather bellowing), was all at once hit by a tremendous idea, with terrifying effect on a herd of cattle – whereupon he was himself driven from the field by an angry herdsman who thought him an escaped lunatic. There are plenty of unsubstantiated anecdotes about Beethoven; but the finale of the Eighth is suspiciously like internal evidence for this one.

Symphony No. 9, in D Minor

The proper title of the Ninth is 'Symphony with final chorus on Schiller's Ode to Joy', an unwieldy mouthful, but better than the vulgarly objectionable English habit of calling it 'The Choral'. It would not be wide of the mark to say that Beethoven's choral symphony is the Mass in D, not this predominantly orchestral work, the character of which has led to vociferous objections to the nature of the finale. Most of the criticism that has been levelled at the choral movement has been rooted, often unconsciously, in the kind of purism that will not admit the possibility of words and voices at a late stage in an instrumental composition, and it is important to remember that when we refer to the Ninth as the 'Choral' Symphony we are crudely recognising the dramatic power of the human voice to throw everything else, no matter how impressive, into the background. So far as I know, no one has ever attempted a symphony with a choral first movement followed by three instrumental ones. If we make the effort (some may think, pedantically) to avoid regarding the Ninth as Beethoven's choral symphony, we can at least be sure of getting the perspective right. It is important to do so, for most of the criticisms that have been levelled at the work arise from failure in this respect.

The purist notion abhors all hybrids, but is as sure to result in degeneracy as the sort of in-breeding that causes mental deficiency, certainly if the purism is concentrated on mere materials; the idea of an 'orchestra' or a 'choir' is a mere abstraction until the composer's imagination animates it, and once this process of animation has begun the matter of purity is something for the artist's instinct alone to judge. If we think ourselves capable of criticising the Ninth Symphony we should at least be careful not to inform Beethoven of what he ought to have avoided; we can learn more by taking it for granted that at this time of his life he had some positive aim that sprang from his nature and his experience, to say nothing of an incomparable genius that was at the zenith of its powers. By this time Beethoven was ready for the almightiest risk of his life. He was also at the stage when his experience told him exactly what risks he could or could not take. Not being infallible he had his doubts, even after the event, and it is perhaps a pity that he voiced them. That he intended at first to give the symphony an instrumental finale is well known, but there is no sadder spectacle than the alacrity with which a critic will quote his victim in support of himself; he will agree with a composer's doubts, but will rarely fail to question his expressions of satisfaction. That is one reason why composers are so often reluctant to comment on their own works.

To understand why the Ninth has a vocal finale we must first get rid of an ancient fallacy, that a great work of music contains its one-and-only necessary conclusion implied in its beginning. When Berlioz said that once you had the beginning right the rest followed more easily, he did not mean that it came automatically or that there were no alternatives. Too many analysts are bent on demonstrating the inevitability of a work in terms of the exclusion of all other possibilities, a doctrine of which Schoenberg is not innocent, while Schenker builds many a dungeon in the air by means of these principles. Most such thinkers are logic-bound: when they use the word 'logic' they refer to their own ingenuity. They can prove the inevitability of any work they admire by a beautiful process of rationalised wishful thinking, the converse of which enables them as often to demonstrate how a given composer (whom they do not admire) has failed to find this mysterious passage to the truth. The claim that a masterpiece pursues but one possible course is very useful as a weapon against music one does not like. The one truly inevitable thing about a piece of music is the silence after the last note, and the habits of present-day audiences are rendering even this more than uncertain.

It is fascinating to contemplate, in this case, what kind of instrumental movement Beethoven at first thought of as a possible finale for the Ninth Symphony. No two movements could be more different from each other than the finale of the A minor Quartet, Op. 132, and the Ode to Joy, the one rent with impassioned pathos, the other alight with confidence. Yet the sketches show that the quartet movement, or at least its thematic material, was for some time intended for the symphony, and the recitatives occur in both works. These last are modified and made pathetic in the quartet: but even if we ignore them we still cannot say that the rest of the material could have become *only* a quartet, for this would be to fall into the old 'logical' error. Music and logic do not chime together. The real trouble is that the choral finale of the symphony is so familiar that it is hard to imagine anything else, let alone something so utterly opposed to it.

But it is surely possible (and the evidence suggests that Beethoven must have felt it so) that the situation produced by the first three movements of the Ninth might have given rise to a negative rather than a positive reaction. It is not improbable that Beethoven fought severe battles with himself before deciding the matter. The fathomless immensity of the universe can evoke a wide range of human responses, from despair and horror to exultation; what Beethoven must have felt in creating the stupendous first three movements is a matter for conjecture alone, but there can be no doubt that the state of mind that produced them was both exalted and of rare objectivity, beyond ordinary workaday human emotions. The *adagio* seems to prepare the way, by its access of emotional warmth, for the world of human activity. But in what light shall this activity be shown? Shall the domain of men appear little, pathetic, irretrievably riven, a terrible contrast to all this majesty? Beethoven of all people must have known with frightful immediacy the human mind's deep need of genuine heroism to face the fact of its own imagination. In the *Eroica* he had expressed heroism within the orbit of human affairs; but another kind is required here, nothing less than an answer to the challenge man makes to himself when he is at last aware of a seemingly pitiless universe. It would be presumptuous to try to impute this idea to the conscious Beethoven. But the greatest art inevitably reminds us of awesome matters, and there is no doubt, if a wide consensus of instinctive responses is of any account, that the first three movements of the Ninth Symphony spring from regions of the mind not directly involved with the emotional stresses of daily life.

The grandeur of these movements is comprehensive; someone once described the Ninth as a work for orchestral tutti, presumably meaning that the musical burden was evenly borne by the whole orchestral apparatus; however varied Beethoven's scoring the *melos* is at all times widely distributed. The result is an absence of deliberately individual treatment of instruments; solo passages quickly merge again into the whole, a good example being the famous D major horn passage in the coda of the first movement:

Ex. 35

p dolce

On the other hand this situation produces a striking individualisation of the whole orchestra as such, which becomes a consistent world in itself. The listener is faced with a self-contained phenomenon, as detached as the stars in their courses, and as far beyond the noisy traffic of everyday life. A similar impression can be had from some of Bach's fugues, and there is significance in this. The widely diffused *melos* of the orchestra becomes itself a polyphony, and the immensity is sensed as almost static by the diminutive human observer. We move while the sky appears to stand still, but our movement is as nothing compared with the real motion of the stars and galaxies. Beethoven's genius was so naturally dramatic (in normal human terms) that it took him nearly all his life to reach this point. The drama, far from being lessened, now becomes more comprehensive. The orchestral tutti is a kind of polyphony that is dramatic as a totality, as the universe itself is dramatic in a way that transcends its spectacular but minor details.

Beethoven's treatment of the orchestra in these first three movements, together with the character of his musical invention, at once creates an awe akin to that of contemplating the sky; the Ninth Symphony, so far, is fundamentally a contemplative work on a plane of imagination possible to few at first hand, but available to many at the instigation of the few. This kind of imagination can be so overwhelming as to evoke either exaltation or despair; the latter is more common, but the former is more realistic because the human creature, at least in its own sphere of knowledge, is the only one capable of such imagination. Imagination is one thing; contemplation of it is another higher form of imagination, and even if it reaches self-defeating limits is itself as marvellous as the infinities that defeat it. At this point marvelling often ceases and despair sets in, and it is here that Beethoven proves himself the objective realist rather than the mechanically emoting romantic. It is at this point that the highest type of heroism must be summoned; when man reels at the impact of his own imagination let him contemplate with awe and joy those very powers with which he is able to stagger himself. They, too, are part of the whole. So the joy is profoundly reasonable, and Beethoven says in effect, 'The visions of the first three movements are such as to reduce man to the apparent size of a microbe; but a man conceived them, so let us all rejoice in our potentialities.' From the thought of an immense and enigmatic universe we turn, impelled by a growing reassurance in the *adagio*, to an arena brilliantly lit by man, the gleam of whose intelligence and imagination causes the twinkling stars and the pale moon to fade from the eye. What could be more natural than that this work should end with human voices? Natural, but (it is necessary to repeat) not inevitable. That it ends thus is due to Beethoven's choice at that time between two opposites. In the A minor Quartet he explored the other, and even there he could not allow the despair to win.

Any criticism of the finale of the Ninth must confine itself to the musical achievement. To complain that it is choral is as futile as to call a concerto cadenza an excrescence simply because the orchestra is not playing. The cadenza is either organic and natural or it is not. For me, as I hope I have shown, the choral finale is the natural outcome of the rest, and I find it as a composition magnificent. Its structure is both subtle and strong, and its precursor, the finale of the *Eroica*, has been almost equally misunderstood. The last movement of the Ninth is an organic blend of variations and sonata, with both introduction and symphonic coda, and not without a suggestion of rondo. Structurally it is a summing-up of classical possibilities, all expressed in a single huge design with astonishing certainty of touch; it has even the shade of the classical concerto in it, as if Beethoven, like Bach in *The Art of Fugue*, were intent on encompassing everything he knew in one mighty act. It is this extraordinary comprehensiveness of suggestion in the finale that enables Beethoven to place it after the *adagio*, which also makes variations one of its central issues. It is difficult to think of another symphony with two successive movements that give prominence to variations. This is the final expression of that immensely static quality already mentioned, with the triumphant added subtlety that the growth of the symphony towards the specifically human impels Beethoven to convey the final variation movement upon the current of a vast sonata process; the two elements miraculously interpenetrate. He had anticipated the idea in the underrated Choral Fantasia fifteen years earlier, as well as in the *Eroica* finale before that; it now reaches its supreme expression when the greatest of all Beethoven's orchestral music is compelled to retire into the background. *Adagio* and finale are complementary in the sense that one suggests the other; as the growing human warmth of the slow movement turns our attention gradually from cosmic nature to the place of man, so its very form hints at the finale, which somehow reconciles the static quality of variations with the active forces that inform humanity and are most aptly conveyed by sonata-music. The *adagio*, moreover, with its alternating themes and the mighty slow dynamic of the gigantic modulations on which its life is based, is not inactive; in it the spirit prepares itself for action.

It remains to consider the first two movements. For Beethoven, as for any great classical composer, the distinction between an introduction and a real beginning was always acute. It would be fascinating to devise a theory that would explain what it is that causes some allegros to have introductions and some not. I have already made the point that it took Beethoven a long time before he began a first movement, without an introduction, with a self-contained tune; to start thus bluntly needs tremendous authority and the unerring ability to develop momentum immediately. An introduction can create an impressive atmosphere in the shadow of which the simplest things can seem more significant that they would if they were unprepared. Try to imagine the Seventh Symphony if it began with the flute solo at the opening of the *vivace*! The aura in which we perceive this innocent melody is entirely created by the introduction. The surest way to find out if an introduction is necessary is to imagine the piece without it, and if this observation seems platitudinous, it at least shows a clear idea that introductions and beginnings are distinct things, which is something a great many romantic composers seem not to have understood. As so often, they have been misled by Beethoven, whom they mistakenly regarded as their romantic mentor, giving them by his example permission to obscure as many artistic issues as they wish by the use of magnificent emotional gestures. Nothing could be more apparently introductory than the beginning of the Ninth Symphony, which is like the genesis of music itself, and nothing could be more truly a real beginning, as we can perceive when the rhythmic fragments have gathered themselves into a tremendous unison theme. For the first time in music (one is tempted to say, for the only time) the two contradictory functions are inextricably fused, and there never was an opening more frequently, or less successfully, imitated than this. The sketches show that Beethoven had the whole idea in his head from the start; the fragment of rhythm is jotted down before the whole subject, and the process of composition was a matter of working out the exact proportions that would produce perfect delivery of the unison theme. No other composer who has attempted such an opening has possessed Beethoven's sense of proportions, or the ability to generate the whole thing twice in quick succession, the second time viewed from a different tonal angle, that of the submediant, B flat.

What Beethoven had discovered about tonality in the Seventh Symphony now makes it possible for him to anticipate, with enormous emphasis, the key of his second group in the middle of his first; this is because B flat is first approached as part of D minor, as D minor is at first approached through a misty A, each event secured by means of primitive genius (bassoons and horns first dropping to D against the held A, then later, after preparation on D and A, establishing a triad of B flat with the woodwind just before the main theme breaks out in that key). The colossal anticipation of the key of the second group makes a long transition unnecessary. It is as important not to regard Ex. 36 as the beginning of the second group as it is not to suppose that it anticipates the 'joy' theme in the finale; that is the kind of ingenuity (if such it can be called) that should, but does not, get analysts a bad name.

Ex. 36

p dolce

The second group really begins a few bars later, where Beethoven has considerably put the change of key-signature and a double bar, when the music settles properly in B flat. The whole first movement, with its astounding suggestion of vastness by strictly limited means (its range of modulation, except for a couple of 'Neapolitan' inflexions that are not modulations at all, is less wide than, say, Contrapunctus IV in Bach's *Art of Fugue*), produces a multidimensional effect even more remarkable than that we noticed in the Seventh Symphony, but by the control of movement and dynamics rather than by the schematic use of remote keys. The development, despite its great length and variety of incident, is basically a single vast crescendo, its beginning surpassing in length and mystery the opening of the movement; its culmination is in the flaming supernova explosion of the reprise, in a terrible D major. At the very beginning of the symphony we gaze mystified at a distant nebula, the bare fifth on A and E at the start, and on D and A at bar 36. The development opens with A and E, as if to repeat the exposition, but in bar 170 comes a soft awesome thrill, a quiet chord of D major with its third (F sharp) in the bass. It seems remotely distant (physically, not tonally) but almost menacingly clear. We do not understand that this remote system threatens our own, and the momentary thrill of terror fades into G minor, of which D major is, after all, only the dominant (see bar 178). It is not the least amazing thing in this movement that the tonic major sounds more remote, at times, from the tonic minor than any foreign key. After many other events, when we have almost forgotten about it, we glance at the sky – and it is blazing from horizon to horizon. We are flung into the heart of the fiery D major nebula, and the recapitulation has begun. The whole of the recapitulation is affected by this cataclysm; themes that were openly in the major now fall into a limbo between minor and major; in the coda we are finally overwhelmed beneath a surging groundswell that is anticipated, very differently, in the first movement of the Seventh Symphony at the corresponding point. The first movement of the Eighth Symphony ended with a self-contained thematic figure that had the point of a joke; at the similar place in the Ninth the self-sufficiency of the great theme that closes the movement with such awful punctuality outfaces us with an inexorable enigma.

The scherzo, the greatest of its kind in existence, is the second movement; no longer can it be taken for granted that scherzo and finale complement each other. The natural course of events in the Ninth Symphony ensures that it shall be the *adagio* that eases the way into the last movement; here the scherzo is complementary to the first movement. Had Beethoven been a modern scientist of the widest possible culture as well as a musician of unique genius he could scarcely have expressed his impressions of cosmology and nuclear physics, the two extremes of macrocosmic and microcosmic vastness, with more force and accuracy than in the first two movements of this symphony. By contrast with the first movement the *molto vivace* (*allegro molto vivace* in the manuscript) concentrates on pure energy which, like that trapped in an atom, might well exist indefinitely, until it were released and dissipated. It develops full sonata form and, even so, shows signs of pursuing a 'circular' course like some of its smaller fellows. The composer remains content with the suggestion, for how could such energy be stopped if its implications were allowed literal fulfilment? Beethoven possessed a power of movement greater than any other composer's; here it attains its utmost expression, and the athletic motion of sonata is marvellously enhanced by wonderful polyphony that makes the whole seem uncannily poised. It is perhaps unlikely that Rossini appreciated the full significance and power of this movement, but the sheer beautiful energy of it can make one sympathise with his delightfully characteristic observation that the scherzo, of course, was inimitable, but as for the rest of the work, it lacked charm. Beethoven's trio, for the first time in the symphony, seems to be ordinary human music; but its sense of delight does not comprehend the enormous forces pent in the scherzo – to a child a pantomime fairy is as magical as a real one, and the gaiety of the trio is as real as a child would think it. And a man is a child in the face of things that are either too vast or too minute for him to grasp – or so it is at this stage in the Ninth Symphony. This trio, moreover, is in D major; in the first movement the sound of the major mode was as a flaming cosmic catastrophe, terrible and almost unimaginable; here it is entrancing and delightful – a child might not see much difference between photographs of the Crab Nebula and an exploding rocket. It is not until the last movement that the major mode comes to mean something that includes both points of view – a gross mistranslation of Schiller might indicate that by his (Beethoven's) magic is united what this mode had parted wide.[1]

Ex. 37

---

1 With apologies to the translation by Natalia Macfarren.